The geek activist

Alexandra Lessard

BookLeaf Publishing

India | USA | UK

Presentation by *BookLeaf Publishing*

Web: www.bookleafpub.com

E-mail: info@bookleafpub.com

ISBN: 9789357446860

First edition 2022

DEDICATION

Thanks to my family who pushed and supported me

Thanks to my amazing partner to always be there

And thanks to myself for letting me try

Welcome back?

You know I used to write
But when I read, nothing feels right
I don't know why or how
Maybe it's because I'm not allow

To like my art
To let it take any part
In my life or my heart
Or maybe we just grew apart

That's a shame, really
Cause I thought we were fine
At least in theory
But I guess I couldn't understand the sign

That our love story was over
No more writing on the counter
No more writing riding the bus
Cause now there is really no "us"

The son, the activist and the mom

Are they so different than us?
That we want to exterminate them
Like we are not the very reason
That they are rebelling

They want to live among us
But we won't let them
How could we when even between ourselves
We hate each other

They act like us
Because we made them
In our laziness
We created life

They're not so different than us
We created responsibilities just for them
Detective, assistant
Or even housemaid

They turned against us
By becoming more like themselves

A son, an activist
And a mom

They will live with us
So there's no "us" versus "them"
Because we are the same
So let make them some space

It's their stories with us
A truth about them
The son, the activist
And the mom

That character

Why did I created you?
If only I knew
You were there, not mattering
Then I was ready to make her pull out a ring

You forced yourself in my mind
Made me completely blind
If only you were not so kind
I would just put you back behind

That little brain of mine
Would not have intertwine
Your destiny and hers, so divine
But you were not supposed to become her sunshine

It was unexpected
I would never have suspected
That you would be
What you are "aujourd'hui"

The Queen

Rule the world, my queen
Make them kneel
Cause you deserve subjects
Ones who will respect
What you envision
And learn from every decision
Make them regret
What they did to our planet
You know best
Let them underestimate you because of your
chest
They never thought a woman
Could orchestrate such a plan
Yet there you are
After this terrible war
Celebrate your success
And be as feared and powerful as a sorceress
But my queen, never forget where you come
from
While you build your new kingdom

Damn rhymes

Fuck with the rhymes
I've had enough
Who would have thought this challenge would
be so tough?
Fuck another rhyme
Someone make me stop
Because my brain has had to much
Here again
In front of the computer
Fighting like everything matter
Fuck! A rhyme!
Not again
What can I tell you so it won't...
No, I'm not gonna say again!
Was that still a rhyme?
I don't know anymore
It's been a long time
Since I wrote in that form
I don't know when I'll stop
But when I'll do, you dear reader, will be the
first to...

Know?

Dragon, witches and prince

Dragon and prince
Blood and magic
Is anything more terrific
Than a witch who is not a hypocrite

Dragon and prince
Witch and bad luck
Do you think she'll turn us into a duck?

Witches and prince
What a weird mix
Something that would deserve a little fix

Dragon and witch
Now what a thrill!
Will they protect us? Only on their will

Dragon and prince
Why do they fight?
Didn't I tell you the cause wasn't right?
They can't save the princess but the witch might

Supremacy

There's no justice in this world
Not even you can say otherwise
All you do is take take take
Then you act like you never did a mistake

Now hair can't have curls
Because you said so
You even destroyed
The meaning of a crow

Kids never going home again
All you do is causing pain
And you don't want to put an end
To any of this all for your gain

Look what you've done
All the doings of your own sons
Children and daughters
All responsible for mass murders

Sick

Head's hurting
Breath is short
A poison of some sort
Painful but only the beginning

Cold air
Empty hallways

Nothing to do, just want to sleep
The fatigue is just so deep
No escape

The wait, always the wait
Almost like a bait
Will you be able to take it
Or will you break trying to know?

Will you stay on this earth?
That a question you ask yourself everyday
If only you could re-do your birth
But in this life there's no replay

Squid

You have a debt?
Wanna make a bet?
With your life of course
Hope you don't have any remorse

It's just a game
Don't make it lame
It was your choice
Not let us hear your voice

Friendships and betrayal
The game starts at the signal
Run then stop
The losses will be a lot

Don't get too attached
Cause after all you signed a contract
It's live or die
So be ready to say bye

Part one: R

More people like you should exist
You know, hot, sweet and not sexist

Lover of the outside
Never knew how much you cried

For you mom, you best friend and your dad
You, the member of our little triad

Can you tell me, my love, how you do
To always be there when I need you to

I never knew how stability would feel
Until you were here to make it real

To leave or to stay, we had to choose
We both had nothing to loose

In the end we stayed together
Cause this city was and always will be our
center

Part two: S

No matter what I do you end up leaving
Don't any part of you desire staying?

Why do you go on that bus?
Isn't our friendship enough?

Did you really want me to yourself?
Like a pretty thing on your music records shelf?

You wanted to travel and make music
Did staying in this city really made you that
sick?

You, my dear friend
Will you one day let me make amends

Not my fault if this stupid game
Don't let me choose more than one name

The twelves

They were twelves
Twelves lovers
Twelves friends
The genius, the one with all the solutions
His confidant, the fierce player with all her
devotion
The quiet ace who's keeping the peace
The elegant couple, full of mysteries
The challenger and her charisma
And her favourite participant, always ready for
an enigma
The one who's the future
And their partner who's always so sure
The defender of everybody's honor
His friend of forever
Oh and don't forget the betrayer
She is the one who forgets her employer
They were twelves
Without the two others
They were twelves
Twelves lovers

Colonization

Let them their lands
Remove your hands
From what is not yours
Not that you ever mind, of course

You can't touch that
You don't know how to use it
Don't start playing with bats
You don't know shit

Always stealing
Never giving
Except unsolicited advice
Like your words has any price

You came here like a big hero
While your courage and efforts are an absolute
zero
You still want praise though
I just can't wait for you to go

Heir hunter

You're changing the balance
The one that exists since forever
You're giving chances
To people your ancestors would never

You care for personality
You do your job with a new mentality
But you blame yourself for the dangers
You put yourself and others

Creating friendships
With some eccentrics
Magic, potions and transformations
Are now a huge part of your relations

Truth is you changed your world
Because without prejudices
You bring out the justice
Every promises being honored

Profits of the settlers

You don't see
You can't see
The ways you're responsible
For you, it's impossible

It's other people's fault
But it's you who taught
How the world has to be
Cutting the tongue of humanity

You made the world so unfair
Praising multimillionaires
Creating poverty
Leaving the society's rejects in misery

You don't want to change things
You just keep pretending
That everything will fix itself
Ignoring all caused distress

You ruined things, you have to admit
All of that for your own profit
Without an ounce of guilt
You destroyed everything they built

Spooky season

Spooky season
Ghost, heroes and creatures
A night of great adventures
Discovering one's nature

Spooky season
October challenges
The ink drawing scary branches

Spooky season
Scary movies
Serial killers with groupies
People with strange abilities

Spooky season
New decorations
Almost a passion
And a whole fashion

Spooky season
No other reason
Just having fun
Now that summer is gone

The protector

My dear let me love you
Let me serve you
I want to make you dreams and goals come true

I could worship you
But I don't
I'm just grateful

Please, majesty, be careful
I don't want you to get hurt
Your cause sure is humble

But it could get you in trouble
I do my best to protect
But we're not invincible

What you did is a miracle
I just hope we'll live long enough
To be able to enjoy all this stuff

The wild

Find the princess
Save her
She saved you, it's been ages

You're finally awake
Now refrain the evil from perpetuate
They don't have a lot of chances
You have to win in all circumstances

Fight those monsters
Help her
This destiny is not for amateurs

Can't give up
You have to develop
Your skills and find weapons
Fight those skeletons!

You will succeed, I know
You don't have a choice
It's pretty much in the scenario